Flowers from [the Ark]

True Stories from the
Homes of L'Arche

Christella Buser

Foreword by Jean Vanier
Afterword by Henri J.M. Nouwen

Paulist Press
New York, NY • Mahwah, NJ

Cover design by Vitale Communications.

The house drawing on the title page was done by Eddie Hutson, L'Arche, Seattle.

Book design by Jay Gribble, C.S.P.

All royalties earned by this book are being donated to
L'Arche International.

Library of Congress Cataloging-in-Publication Data

Buser, Christella, 1924-
  Flowers from the ark : true stories from the homes of l'Arche / Christella Buser ; foreword by Jean Vanier ; afterword by Henri J.M. Nouwen.
      p.   cm.
  ISBN 0-8091-3639-2 (hb : alk. Paper)
  1. Church work with the mentally handicapped—Catholic Church—Anecdotes. 2. Church work with the developmentally disabled—Catholic Church—Anecdotes. 3. Arche (Association)—Anecdotes. 4. Group homes for the mentally handicapped—Anecdotes. 5. Developmentally disabled—Ancedotes. I. Title.
BX2347.8.M4B87   1996
267´.182—dc20   95-49270
                                                        CIP

Published by Paulist Press
997 Macarthur Boulevard
Mahwah, New Jersey 07430

Printed and bound in the
United States of America

DEDICATION

To the men, women and children of L'Arche
whose generous sharing of themselves
has given me, and others, continual life.

ACKNOWLEDGMENT

This book is the creation of many people. There are so many who have contributed to this work that it is impossible to name them all. I would, however, like to express my appreciation to Mary Mark Whitehair, CSJ, for her help, encouragement and enthusiasm and to Vicky Larson for her generosity in typing the manuscript.

FOREWORD

People with disabilities or with developmental difficulties are wonderful people. They do not have the same rational intelligence and capacities as others, but at the same time they do not wear masks. They have less need to prove they are the best. They are more intuitive, spontaneous, and live closer to the heart. These gifts flower when they know they are accepted and appreciated just as they are.

And that is what L'Arche wants to be: A place where people with disabilities are allowed to be themselves, whatever their limitations or weaknesses may be. They can sing and dance and laugh and cry.

L'Arche began in 1964 when I welcomed two disabled men, Raphael and Philippe, from a large institution. The three of us started to live together in a small house in Trosly, a village in northern France. We worked together, we laughed, we fought each other, we learned to forgive each other, we prayed and we celebrated life together. People came to help us and we were able to welcome more people from institutions and the community grew. There are now some twenty homes in five different villages which make up the first community of L'Arche. From this original community of L'Arche, over a hundred others have sprung up in twenty-six countries.

At the heart of each community there are men and women with disabilities. With them are other men and women who felt attracted by their inner beauty and who came to share their lives with them.

The stories in this book flow from our community, from our daily life together. They are like simple songs of love.

I am grateful to Christella for putting them together. They reveal the beauty of our people. They are a reminder that our people have a simple message of love to give the world today, if people will take the time to listen to them.

Jean Vanier

INTRODUCTION

The birth of this book came about after a L'Arche International Council meeting on a Sunday afternoon in France. Jean Vanier, founder of L'Arche, and I were driving in a small French car to have dinner with the L'Arche community in Boulogne, just across from the English Channel. Little had I realized how fast the people in France drove, and what a surprise to find the roads so full of curves.

A bit frightened and hoping to slow the driver down, I began to tell Jean stories about the men and women with whom I was living in the Winnipeg, Canada, community. After a few stories, Jean, in his thought-provoking way, slowed the car almost to a halt, and suggested I write a simple book of *fioretti*, like the stories told about St. Francis of Assisi after his death. This was the beginning.

For me and the assistants I work with, the core members* have become "wise teachers." They are people versed in grief and grace, and

3

they reflect the image of a loving God. They have a mission to give life, to heal and liberate.

When we get together at various L'Arche events we always exchange L'Arche stories about core members that are sad, joyful, humorous, celebrative and inspirational. Stories like these.

In creating this book, I want to show living examples of what Jean Vanier meant when he said, "Persons with disabilities are prophets of our time, if only we take time to listen to them."

The stories I have written and collected are from some of the L'Arche homes around the world. Each community is unique in its own culture, but the L'Arche spirit remains the same. Read the stories slowly and prayerfully. You will find wisdom in them and laughter to lighten your spirit. It is my fond hope that you will experience the same feelings of joy and sorrow, of pain and delight that I felt in writing this book.

Christella Buser, CSJ

---

* "Core members" is a L'Arche term for community people with disabilities. "Assistants" is our term for those who come to live, help and work in the community.

❦ Sometimes...

Sometimes I wish I could run
   through the fields and
   meadows—without a watch to
   keep time—all by myself—with
   only my thoughts—my
   innermost longings.

Sometimes I wish I could break out
   of my limits, get away from
   duties—just for a few hours.

Sometimes I wish I could run with
   my face to the wind—feeling its
   freshness and freedom—run in
   the sunshine—taking its strength
   and warmth.

Sometimes I wish I could have just a
   little freedom—just for a few
   hours.

I wish I could run in the sun and
   the wind and pick a handful of
   flowers for you in the meadow.

Anne Stewart, assistant
L'Arche, Germany

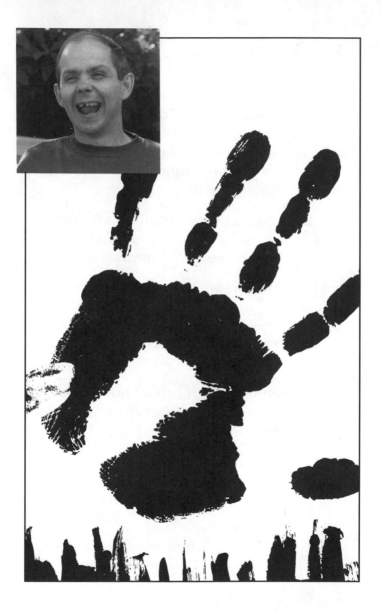

🐎 Cracked Eggs

At Daybreak we used to operate a farm, including an egg operation. The eggs were sold in town, but we kept the ones that were cracked during the packaging process for our own use in the community. One day Len, the farm manager, asked Jim to bring three dozen cracked eggs to the house. Jim said he'd be right down. When it took Jim a long time to appear, Len asked: "What took you so long?" Jim replied, "We were out of cracked eggs, so I had to crack three dozen for you."

L'Arche, Toronto

🐎 Conversational Topic

Dania had spent years in a psychiatric hospital. At 17 years of age she was welcomed into our community. Living with us, she developed a loving relationship with Jesus. It was important for her to focus on the essential. Eventually she began a long physical decline that led to her death. Two days before she died,

Margarita, one of our neighbors, came to visit her. There were three of us in the sickroom, but the conversation was confined to Margarita and myself. After a while, Margarita said to Dania, laughing: "Come on, Dania, what do you want to talk about?" Very seriously Dania raised her head and said, "About Jesus." Our chatter was rebuked, and Dania returned to her silence.

L'Arche, Mexico

❧ The Poor Near at Hand

Money is important to Leonard, and he works hard to earn his paycheck of $10.00 every two weeks. On Monday afternoon he goes to the bank to cash his check. Just for fun one of the assistants in the house used to wait for him and beg for money. On one occasion she got down on her knees and pleaded with Leonard to donate money for a poor old lady. Leonard looked down at her solemnly and announced, "I am the poor."

L'Arche, Mobile

❧ When God Holds You Tight

Every Monday night the whole community comes together for prayer and reflection, during which Pat always reads one page from Jean Vanier's book *I Meet Jesus*. One night after the reading he observed, "You notice the word 'love' occurs three times. Can anyone tell me what love is?" There was dead silence. Finally Dovie, a handicapped core member, answered, "Love is when God holds you tight." Pat asked, "Shall we demonstrate?" Dovie replied: "Sure. Which one of us is going to be God?"

L'Arche, Calgary

❧ Wake Up

Whenever we attended a wake at a funeral home, Denis always announced that he had gone to a "wake up."

L'Arche, Overland Park, Kans.

🐝 Revelation

After two years at Daybreak, I decided to leave. It was a difficult decision to make, especially because of my close relationship with David. I avoided telling David until last because I didn't know how to do it well. Finally we sat down to talk and I told David my news. After a while we both had tears in our eyes. David said, "Wait here, I have something to give you." He came back with a picture of himself when he was eight years old. He said to me, "You're like a brother to me, and I want you to have this picture so you'll never forget me. I want a picture of you so I won't ever forget you." At that moment I knew I would come back to Daybreak. Today I would say that David revealed my vocation to me. Eighteen years later I still carry his picture in my wallet and look at it from time to time, especially when I'm experiencing a difficult moment in community life.

L'Arche, Toronto

🐦 The Catholic Pope

Fred, who was living at Hilltop House with Father David, Father Peter and Father Jim, heard that Pope John Paul I had died. He said, "It's very sad. The Catholics lost their Pope. Do we know any Catholics?"

L'Arche, Tacoma

🐦 Teachers and Learners

Jean Michel, a young retarded man at L'Arche in France, once asked Jean Vanier to talk about community. He wanted to know, "How do we live together?" Vanier answered, "Perhaps it is you, Jean Michel, who should tell us how we live together." Vanier's reply has been my experience. Living at L'Arche has been an experience of learning from the Jean Michels of this world, living close to the moment, trying to extract its essential gift, and then accepting it, integrating it, loving it. It's terribly idealistic, and the reality is always far from the ideal, but for me the challenge is true, and the experience profound.

L'Arche, France

🦋 Birthday Gift

Janet was celebrating her birthday in the L'Arche community, opening her gifts and cards. She said, "Mom and Dad, you gave me a card just like this last year." Janet's mother said, "Oh dear, I'm sure it wasn't the same." Janet marched upstairs and came down with last year's card. Sure enough, it was the same one.

L'Arche, Overland Park, Kans.

🦋 A Question of Marriage

One day a visitor asked Marcia if she would ever like to get married. "Oh, no! Never!" she replied. "I prefer remaining a widow."

L'Arche, Honduras

🦋 Healing Guide

Mike is unable to speak, communicating for the most part by grunts. Shortly after I came home from surgery I was invited to Mike's community for tea. Although I accepted, I began feeling weak with all the people fussing over me. Mike detected my discomfort and tugged at my sleeve to follow him. He led me into the chapel and pointed to the floor. Obediently I sat down, realizing at that moment that Mike knew better than I did what I really needed.

L'Arche, Ottawa

✺ Helping Hand

I first met Hazel fifteen years ago when I was a brand-new assistant at Rosseau Court. She was pleasant to be with, so I made a point of sitting next to her at dinner. Before the meal we prayed holding hands, but as Hazel took my hand I found myself pulling away. I hadn't noticed before that her fingers were joined together. Aware of what I was doing, I tried to stop. Before I could do anything Hazel leaned over and in a soft voice said "Don't worry. You'll be okay." I had come to L'Arche wanting to do all sorts of things for the disabled, only to find I had much to learn from those who are differently abled. Hazel's words freed me from the fears and inabilities that I brought, helping me to rediscover myself in relation to others. I am grateful to the hand that held me, the voice that encouraged me to trust the gifts that are offered in everyday life.

L'Arche, Winnipeg

🐝 Messages

Assistant: Pierre, do you pray?
Pierre: Of course.
Assistant: And what do you say to Jesus?
Pierre: I tell him that I love him.
Assistant: And what does he say to you?
Pierre: He says, "You are my beloved, I love you too."

L'Arche, Switzerland

🐝 The Greatest Fear

Larry used to attend a local church with a neighbor who would drive by to pick him up. One Sunday evening at church a young preacher was putting a lot into his sermon. At one point he asked the rhetorical question "What is your greatest fear?" Our neighbor heard Larry mumbling to himself. Later the minister came back to his question and asked "What is your greatest fear?" In a loud voice Larry called out: "Grizzly bears!"

L'Arche, Frontenac, Ont.

❧ The Visitor

I had recently arrived in the community and found myself troubled by a suspicious looking man who wandered into our garden and was peering in the window. I was ready to go out and challenge the stranger when Bill, our oldest core member, came into the room. I asked Bill if he knew the intruder. Without bothering to check, Bill spread his arms wide and said, "It might be the Lord himself." With a lighter heart I went into the garden and found the visitor belonged to a nearby home for people with learning disabilities.

L'Arche, England

❦ A Matter of Identity

When Dennis was told it was a vegetarian meal, he responded, "I'm not a vegetarian. I'm an American."

L'Arche, Tacoma

❦ One of Many

Mike was asked to be part of the Maundy Thursday footwashing rite at the church. He inquired, "Will I be there by myself?"

"No," said an assistant, "there will be thirteen of you."

"Thirteen of me? Oh, brudder!"

L'Arche, Toronto

❦ Ailing Angel

An assistant told me he thought Bill was sick, and as the doctor for some of the resident members I went to see him, thinking he might be faking in order to get out of work. He hugged me as usual but was clearly feverish. When I read his temperature at 104°, I knew he was truly sick. At the hospital emergency room it was discovered Bill had a dangerous infection of the epiglottis, the flapper valve that separates food going to the stomach from air to the lungs. When infected, it can close off the windpipe suddenly, so it would be necessary to insert a plastic tube under anesthesia to keep the airway open. Bill was taken into surgery, and as we placed him on the operating table I announced to the operating team that Bill was an angel. They eyed me skeptically. We left the room, scrubbed up, and then returned, ready to start. Just then Bill sat up on the table. He motioned us away, bent his head over folded hands and prayed for a full minute as we stood by. He then laid down, arms spread like a cross, and announced, "Go ahead." It was several moments before any of the awed team could proceed.

L'Arche, Tacoma

❧ A Virgin Named Patience

Patty is a talkative person who loves having long conversations with people who are helping her. One day while I was washing her hair she went on and on about the patience it took to deal with an aunt of hers. At last she declared, "You know what they always say: 'Patience is a virgin.'"

L'Arche, Syracuse

❧ A Beatitude

Mike Cooper is 35 years old. He doesn't read, but he loves music, enjoys church services and at evening prayers can often be heard mumbling prayers which are rarely understandable but no less reverent. His favorite phrase is "Jesus make happy." There are moments, in fact, when Mike utters truly astonishing words, like the evening when I called people to prayer. Mike walked to the fireplace mantel, picked up the bible and "read" from it, saying, "A reading from the

book of Hebrews, "Blessed are the baptized."
He then replaced the book and returned to his
seat. The rest of us sat in awed silence, moved
by the powerful "reading" from a person who
doesn't read but listens well and keeps a lot in
his heart.

L'Arche, Clinton, Iowa

ᓭ A Promise

During Barbara's last illness, Mary, a member of our community for nine years, paced
around the sickroom looking at Barbara's
clothes and objects on the dresser. At last she
faced Barbara. "What's going to happen to all
these things?" she asked. "You're going to die
aren't you? What's going to happen to your
dog?" Barbara replied, "I don't know.
Someone will take care of her." Immediately
Mary promised, "I'd like to do that for you."

L'Arche, Erie, Penn.

🎗 A Question of Sharing

Sue, Richard and some others were on a pilgrimage to Lourdes. After a meal on the airplane, Richard wanted to brush his teeth. Sue told him, "But, Richard, we packed your toothbrush."

"What about this one?"

"Richard, that's my toothbrush!"

"I'll rinse it off."

Across the aisle, Father David remarked, "Father Peter borrows mine all the time."

Father Jim, sitting behind him, said, "There's no one in the world I would share my toothbrush with."

Sue gave her toothbrush to Richard.

L'Arche, Seattle

🎗 Accepting Limitations

When Ken's family approached us about his coming to live at L'Arche, we told them our policy required a family visit before deciding. Apparently they didn't understand, because they showed up with Ken and all of his baggage. They were anxious about the transition and were relieved to discover this must be a visit. While they were there, we filled out the application forms, Ken answering most of the medical questions himself. "Ken," I said, "it looks as if you're a healthy man." "I'm in great shape," he replied. "Hardly anything wrong with me except a little bit of brain damage." His ability to see and live the truth was the gift Ken brought with him to L'Arche.

L'Arche, Frontenac, Ont.

🐝 A Matter of Ownership

During the course of a retreat, Joe was looking at old photographs and came across one of him that was taken the day he arrived at our community. A little perplexed with the picture, he turned to his friend beside him and asked, "Maria, who owns that face in my head?"

L'Arche, Ireland

♪⑥ Night Watcher

I heard Carole prancing around upstairs after 11:00 p.m. The next morning Fran told me Carole had hardly slept. When I confronted Carole with this and asked her what she was doing, Carole—with a stutter to get out the first words—replied with a sneaky grin, "I was just checkin' up on ya."

L'Arche, Boston

♪⑥ The First Thing To Do

Marjorie, a longtime friend and member of our community, was living with her stepfather, Vic, at the time of his death. We all assumed Marjorie would move in with us when that happened. So when Marjorie phoned Debbie, our director, with news of Vic's death, Debbie made it clear that a place was waiting for her. Marjorie was distraught, crying, "Oh, what am I going to do? What am I going to do?" Debbie assured her, saying, "Marjorie, you know you always have a home here at Noah Sealth." But Marjorie wouldn't be calmed down. She continued to cry, "What am I going to do? What am I going to do?" When Debbie persisted in laying out plans for the future, Marjorie interrupted, "No, stupid...with the body!"

L'Arche, Seattle

🐝 An Important Consideration

Because Patsy dearly wanted to go shopping on her own, Liz spent a great deal of time teaching her about money. They talked one day about the relationship between a ten dollar bill and two five dollar bills. Liz used an example: "Now, Patsy, let's say you wanted to buy a sweater that cost ten dollars. You can give the saleslady a ten dollar bill and she'll give you the sweater, or you can give her two five dollar bills and she'll give you the sweater. Is that clear? Do you have any questions?" "Yes," said Patsy. "What color is the sweater?"

L'Arche, Toronto

🌿 The Comforter

Marcel and I had gone to see the film, *Julia*. I was crying as the movie progressed, and Marcel leaned over to remind me, "Chris, this is only a movie." At the end I was still wiping my eyes. Marcel comforted me, saying, "Chris, I'll be glad to wait a few minutes before we leave the theater."

L'Arche, Winnipeg

🌿 Theologian

The conversation took place just before prayer at Arch I.

Joe: Who's God, Dan?
Dan: [thoughtfully] God?...God's a man.
Joe: He is?
Dan: God don't need no car, Joe. [silence] Anyway, God only rides to the cemetery in a hearse. [another silence] There are many kinds of hearses—Chevys, Fords, Lincolns, Cadillacs, Jaguars...Jaguar is a good hearse.

[another silence] I wish I was a funeral home man. I'd give God a ride to the cemetery.

L'Arche, Clinton, Iowa

🐦 Success Story

Jean-Marc, who was classified "irretrievable" because of his IQ, now lives on his own, manages his own budget, invites his friends to visit and radiates a real sense of welcome.

L'Arche, France

🐦 Canticle for Delores

When Delores first came to L'Arche six years ago you couldn't get near her. She used to pace around the dining room table in an agitated manner. She rarely spoke, and when she did she would disparage herself. She referred to herself as "she" or "this one here." The times I spent with her were often unpleasant. Helping Delores bathe was a special challenge because she would constantly stand up in the tub and ask, "Done yet? Done yet?" She never called me by my name—Mary Therese—and instead called me Mary Tricia, which she still does today. She would say, "Don't want Mary Tricia." This happened so often I was hurt. I was doing everything for her, yet she seemed to hate me.

Slowly, very slowly, the change began between Delores and me. I love songs and would sing a funny little song to her: "Can do, can do, we know that the horse can do." The "can do" counterbalanced Delores' belief that "she can't." Once I did a funny little dance while singing, and something wonderful happened: Delores smiled. Eventually she laughed, got up and danced with me. Little by little we began growing together. She'd ask for me when I was away; when she'd hear my voice in a group, she would smile. Trust, however, wasn't easy for Delores. She was afraid when she had to go out somewhere and would keep asking "Coming back home?" She had to learn that she could go out with others and they would bring her back. These days Delores has gone out of town on retreats and has visited an assistant's home for a weekend. She gives kisses and hugs, and she loves going shopping.

As caregivers come and go, Delores' walls start going up again, but not as much as before. She's learning that life goes on, and she knows that she's loved. She's also becoming more independent. Before, if you told her to sit down she'd sit in that place forever, without even thinking of moving. Now she follows us from room to room and enjoys being with people. It used to be, when someone came to wake her from a nap, Delores would jump right up. When I asked one day whether she wanted to get up, Delores replied, "Not yet." What a joy. What a triumph for Delores. I am grateful for the gift of herself. She has taught me gentleness, showed me beauty, and is teaching me more about love every day.

L'Arche, Erie, Penn.

🐾 The Proper Use of Money

In Madras, the men's salaries used to be put in the bank on Friday, but each was given 10 paisa (about 5 centimes) for himself. Jagakumat would go to the village and buy a small biscuit with his money. Then with delight he would break it into crumbs and give everyone a bite.

L'Arche, India

❧ Forgiveness

Pierre was a very gentle man with a particular dread of violence in any form. One day while taking a walk he was threatened by Jeffrey, a fellow resident whose perpetual anguish seemed always on the brink of explosion. The encounter left Pierre trembling with fear for hours afterward. At evening prayer, although he was still shaking, Pierre said, "Lord, I pray for Jeffrey because there is a lot of pain in him." We were struck by the ease with which Pierre moved from fear to forgiveness after an incident that would have left most of us resentful for days or weeks.

L'Arche, Switzerland

❧ Angel Eyes

Rosie's tiny body is rigid and contorted when she's awake, but relaxes when she's asleep or taking a bath. Her eyes, though, are beautiful—brown tinged with green, and brilliant, like windows to her heart. I have the great fortune from time to time to waken Rosie, bathe her and feed her breakfast. The experience is always moving. After preparing her bath, I go into Rosie's room and call her. Her body is peaceful. Her beautiful eyes open with a look of tenderness and light. For me, it is like being in the presence of an angel. I give thanks for the opportunity to receive this light that is so freely given.

L'Arche, Calgary

✎ Real Medicine

Janet was attending the Special Olympics when she fell from the top of a bunk bed, suffered a concussion, and went into a coma. For some time she was in intensive care. At Janet's house there was a discussion around the breakfast table.

"I sure wish Janet would come home," said Matt.

"But Matt," Denis replied, "she needs the nurse to give her medicine and IV's."

"I know that," said Matt. "But we could give her love."

L'Arche, Overland Park, Kans.

🐝 Missed Opportunity

Luisito was the first person welcomed into L'Arche in Santo Domingo. He had spent his earlier life on the streets without adequate clothing or food. He often sat on our front porch, rocking back and forth, sometimes pounding his chest. A poor laborer used to stand under a tree by our house, a sickle in his hands, waiting for work. For hours he would watch Luisito on our porch. One day we hired him to clean weeds around the house, and afterward Maryse brought him food. As he ate he told her that as a baby he had been very sick, but people gave him goat's milk and he got well. Perhaps, he said, if he had not received the goat's milk, he might have grown up an invalid and someone would love him as we loved Luisito.

L'Arche, Santo Domingo

🐝 Simple Acceptance

It was all so very simple. David Rothrock and I were walking down the alley from the old thirteen-bedroom house where we lived. It was there we met Fred and Greg, two men with mental disabilities. We asked them if they would join us for dinner, and they accepted. That was the beginning, as simple as that. The next evening they appeared at our door at dinnertime and shared a second meal. It went on, night after night. After a year we asked them to live with us permanently, and they said yes.

I lived with Fred and Greg for four good—very good—years. I have never since had a comparable experience. There were many happy times, and a few rough, turbulent times. Fred and I were very similar. He was like a mirror held up to my compulsions and weaknesses. I learned a great deal from him and Greg. I never had to perform for them. They just accepted me—as simple as that.

L'Arche, Tacoma

🐜 Phone Call

One year when I was away on holidays from Daybreak, I called collect to the community to see whether someone could pick me up at the

airport. David answered the phone, and the operator politely said, "This is a collect call from Joe Egan; will you accept the charge?" David was equally polite and replied, "I'm sorry, but Joe is away." The operator explained, "No, this call is from Joe Egan; will you accept the charge?" David patiently repeated, "I'm sorry, but Joe's not here." At this point I tried to help by saying, "David, it's me, Joe." As the operator was asking me not to speak, David exclaimed, "Oh, Joe, there's a phone call for you!"

L'Arche, Toronto

🐾 Heart Friends

Basil has been a member of our community since 1975. He's a large man with a tender, caring nature. He often visits Annapurna, one of our community households, and sits for hours with Darryl who is profoundly disabled. Basil will put his arm around Darryl and let Darryl's head lay on his breast. They make an icon of communion. Recently Basil and I were discussing Epiphany and the gifts that the kings brought to Jesus. I asked Basil what gift he would like to give Jesus and without hesitation he answered, "My heart."

L'Arche, Calgary

❧ Waiting Period

Beryl, 47, had lived in an institution since he was 17. Our community decided to welcome him as a member. On a stormy day Jim worked late, then drove to the Center to get Beryl. When he saw Beryl waiting with all his worldly possessions—two suitcases and a big bag—Jim said, "I'm sorry I kept you waiting. Have you been here long?" Beryl said, "Yeah, about thirty years."

L'Arche, Edmonton

❧ Chinese Food

I love to play Chinese checkers with Bill, who usually beats me—which is good because he hates to lose. However during one game I was starting to win at last. Then out of the corner of my eye I caught Bill popping a marble into his mouth. The further he fell behind, the more marbles he tried to hide in his mouth. He was getting desperate. I finally challenged him about it. At first he mumbled a strong denial, but then began to pull the marbles out one by one. With a big smile on his face he said, "I wonder how they got in there?"

L'Arche, Toronto

❧ A Welcoming Presence

Debbie, at the Memorial Day parade in Haverhill, shouted and waved with tears in her eyes at the marchers, crying "Welcome home! Welcome home!" Turning to me with a smile of utmost joy and thanksgiving, more tears welling in her eyes, she exulted: "They made it!" She thought they were troops returning from the Gulf War.

L'Arche, Boston

🍒 Labor Recognized

Attending a celebration at St. Mary's Cathedral in Winnipeg, Gerry happened to be at the end of the pew. When Cardinal Flahiff processed down the aisle in full liturgical vesture, Gerry stepped out of the pew and said "Evening, bishop. I see you have your work clothes on tonight."

L'Arche, Winnipeg

🍒 Coverup

Packie was in the bath, shouting and yelling, obviously in some difficulty. Olga, just outside the door, told him, "If you come out with a towel wrapped around you, I'll come in." Packie came out with a towel wrapped around his head.

L'Arche, England

❧ The Assistance of Saints

Ernie came to us after having been over-looked in an institution most of his life. Since he was psychotic, he had no sense of relationship with other people and no sense of his own identity. The big thing for him was to become a man. During a homily at mass, the priest said, "This is the feast of St. Joseph. Does anyone know what St. Joseph did?" Ernie's arm shot up, "St. Joseph helped God be a man."

L'Arche, Clinton, Iowa

❧ Danger Perceived

One of the assistants in the community came down with hepatitis. The mother of the assistant was a nurse, so she came to the house with serum to inoculate the assistants and core people. Richard was standing by the door when she arrived. He looked at the equipment she was carrying, cried "I see danger!" and took off.

L'Arche, Seattle

🐦 Mr. Bluebird

As recited by Elsa Mae:

> Good morning, Mr. Bluebird,
> I've come to buy your wings,
> To fly across the ocean
> To hear Miss Lucy sing.
>
> Miss Lucy had a baby
> And everytime he cried,
> She put him in a cradle
> And gave him chicken pie.
>
> Wish I had a nickel,
> Wish I had a dime.
> Wish I had a ginger cake
> To get a bride of mine.

L'Arche, Cleveland

🐦 Farewell Discourse

Everyone knew for weeks that Ellen, one of the assistants, was leaving. Antoinette (Toni) would walk around the house, hands clasped behind her back, brooding about it. She would go into a room where Ellen was and say—not directly to Ellen but to the air—"Don't go. Don't go." At the departure party for Ellen, according to tradition everyone sitting at the table said a few words, everyone but Toni. Finally Toni said, "Oh, let her go. Let her go." Better than anyone, Toni summed up our feelings: "Let her go. We're sorry she's leaving. So let her go."

L'Arche, Frontenac, Ont.

❧ That Guy

During the night a big snow fell on Winnipeg.

Trevor: Ag, come quick. That guy sure blew it last night. Look at all the snow!

Ag: What guy?

Trevor: You know, that guy that brings the sun up here in the morning and takes it down over there at night.

L'Arche, Winnipeg

❧ Parting Gift

At Ron's wake, each member of the community left a red rose in a vase beside the coffin in remembrance of his life with us. Marie Claire was hesitant about coming forward, but later, on her own, she took a rose and went toward the coffin. When she came to the vase she turned to face Ron's parents, walked over and gave her rose to his mother.

L'Arche, Sudbury, Ont.

❧ Only Son

A parents' meeting brought the realization flooding back to Charlie that his mother had rejected him thirty years previously when he was five and had never seen him since. That evening he prayed aloud: "Oh God, help me to find my mother. You know that I am her only son. I'm no good because I can't read or write, but if you help me find my mother she'll recognize me as her only son, and she'll take me back, and she'll say she's sorry she left me."

L'Arche, Toronto

41

🐛 A Disease of Choice

Barbara kept asking to see the doctor. We suspected she was just looking for attention when every night she had a new complaint, but to be safe we made appointments for her. One day she came rushing back from the doctor's office absolutely delighted, crying, "Michael, Michael, the doctor says I have hypochondria!"

L'Arche, England

🐛 An Important Question

During my first year in our community I helped to welcome a man who had been in an institution for sixty-seven years. Everything about L'Arche was a new experience for him. We tried to tell him what to expect when at a meeting we would discuss his habilitation plan for the coming year. He agreed to participate. About forty-five minutes into the meeting, we reviewed with Charlie everything that had been said and reminded him he was free to ask questions of his own. Charlie looked around the table at all the people present—assistants, administrators, program specialist, nurses and supervisors from the workshop. He hesitated. We all waited to hear what was on his mind. Finally he spoke: "So, how are you doing today, Connie?" and gave me his famous smile. "Fine," I quickly mumbled, as laughter filled the room.

L'Arche, Erie, Penn.

✂ Suffering Inside Me

"Hey, Odile, I have suffering inside me and it won't come out," said Daniel, pointing to his chest to show where he was suffering.

"But you're a little better now, aren't you?" I asked him.

"Yes, a little bit." Then he added: "And you, Odile, do you have suffering?"

"Yes," I answered, "I have suffering in me too."

"Then we're the same," he said with a look of sympathy.

L'Arche, France

ᏀᎾ Intercessory Prayer

Whenever Joe is having a difficult time with life, I suggest a drive to Calvary Cemetery and a visit to his mother's grave. Joe was deeply attached to his mother. At the gravesite he can pour out his heart and his grief. This special man has taught me much in the five years I have known him. Most of all, he has taught me how to pray.

L'Arche, Erie, Penn.

ᏀᎾ Information Gap

A retired serviceman and his wife donated a shed to the Heartland community. Several weeks later the community invited them to a "thank you" supper. When the speeches, balloons and ribbon-cutting were finished, our visitor was telling stories of his life while growing up. He told how his mother died shortly after he was born with the result that he never knew her. Suzy, who was listening attentively, commiserated: "Oh, so nobody taught you about the birds and the bees."

L'Arche, Overland Park, Kan.

❧ Conversations of Another Kind

Rita had limited verbal expression and sometimes seemed out of touch with her surroundings. However she loved plants and enjoyed caring for them in the house and on the grounds. One of the assistants who had plants in his room occasionally invited her in to visit. One day he noticed her lips moving as she peered at his plants, and he asked, "Rita, what are you doing?"

"Looking at the plants," she answered.

"Are you talking to the plants?"

"Talking to the plants," she said.

"Are they talking back?"

"Talking back, talking back," said Rita.

"Rita, what are the plants saying?" the assistant asked.

There was a long pause, and then Rita announced, "They say they are growing."

L'Arche, Frontenac, Ont.

❧ A Starting Point

My problem with Paul was always the same. Why doesn't the man shower after finishing work on the farm? I can't enjoy my meal while sitting next to someone who smells like a barnyard. Paul's view is different: If this is his home, and if he is supposed to be himself, then others shouldn't tell him what to do after a long day's work. At the dinner table one night, Paul's odor was especially ripe and I got upset. We had a loud argument, our voices so heated that all other conversation stopped. At last Paul left the table in a huff while the rest of us tried to recreate some semblance of family sharing. After dinner and the dishes, Frank called me aside. He took me to his bedroom where it was quiet and where I might understand him despite his speech difficulties. "I see you are having trouble with Paul," he said. I was defensive and answered, "Never mind that, Frank. Paul and I will work it out." But Frank held me with his eyes and said, "You know, if you want to help Paul, you have to start loving him."

L'Arche, Toronto

♨ Partners on the Road

Ken and I were partners at a L'Arche retreat in Spokane. The theme of the retreat was "Walking Together." Many times since then, in tough times and happy ones, Ken has shown his fidelity to the message of that retreat by reminding me. "Well, Lorne, we're still 'walking together.'"

L'Arche, Vancouver

♨ A Matter of Adoption

Angeline House had two cats that were fine mousers but so haughty in dealings with mere humans that the community got thoroughly tired of them. After the last cat ran away, it was decided "No more cats!" However when Mike was visiting a friend one day, a cat jumped into his lap, sat down and purred. Mike was enchanted. The cat, said Mike's friend, was a stray in need of a home, and immediately Mike wanted to adopt him. He summoned members of the community to consider it. After a long discussion around the dinner table, the vote to adopt the cat was tied at 3 to 3. Dean entered the room late. Mike explained the situation and gave him a chance to break the deadlock. Dean, however, was adamantly opposed to adoption, declaring "I'm sick and tired of cats. They're no good. I want a Doberman!" Mike's face fell, but only for a moment. With a sly grin he suggested, "What if we name the cat Doberman?" It was Dean's turn to grin. "All right," he said. "That's a great idea." And that's the story of how Angeline House got a cat named Doberman and how Dean became its best friend.

L'Arche, Seattle

🐾 The Candidate

Three years ago there was an election to choose regional coordinators of L'Arche, and my name was mentioned as a candidate. I knew the position would require me to spend time away from my job as director of the local house, so I polled members of our community to see if they would support me. Some minded that I'd be traveling, but Robert immediately volunteered, "I'll do your work here." At the eucharist on the following week, Robert petitioned, "I want you to pray because I'm seriously thinking of becoming the director." Only then did I catch on.

L'Arche, Montreal

✸ A Moving Experience

Ian is disabled and suffers from seizures. One night a light earthquake rocked our house and brought Ian to his feet. He told the director, "Brian, this is the first time I was ever awake during a seizure."

L'Arche, Frontenac, Ont.

✸ Him Again

It's springtime, and the buds are beginning to appear on the trees. Trevor calls out, "Ag, look at the buds on those trees. That guy sure knows how to do his magic."

L'Arche, Winnipeg

🎵 Words of Support

In the early morning when passing Frank's door I'd hear him speaking, probably to himself. One morning I stopped and listened. Because Frank's speech is not clear I could make out only a few words—"Jesus... happy...Jesus...Daybreak"—along with the names of people in the community whose problems at the moment were common knowledge.

L'Arche, Toronto

🎵 Evening Prayer

Kevin: O God, bless my Mum, my Dad, my brother Brian, my sister Lisa and my dog Coal. Jesus, you tell Ag I'm sorry about what happened today.

Ag: Kevin, *you* tell me you're sorry.

Kevin: No, Jesus, *you* do it.

L'Arche, Winnipeg

🕊️ A Moment of Grace

Still only a young girl, Judith was welcomed into our community of Tegucigalpa after spending many years in a hospital with her hands bound. She exhibited furious aggression toward herself and everyone taking care of her. We had to bathe, feed and dress her while enduring blows aimed at ourselves and while trying to protect her from the harm she'd do to herself. I couldn't repress feeling resentment at being a target for her hostility, despite my love and compassion for this sad child. To stay within the boundaries of our tolerance, we took turns caring for Judith. I, however, was her designated reference person, her mother image, with whom she might relive the childhood she never had.

One day I was walking toward the house where we lived. It was my turn to take care of Judith and I was reaching my limits of patience. I had had enough of her blows. I didn't want to see her self-inflicted wounds, or listen to the blows she gave herself in her room. I was filled with anger and hostility toward her, and the feelings frightened me. At that moment I felt incapable of dealing with Judith. As I entered the house, though, the feelings suddenly vanished. I was peaceful and relaxed. I couldn't understand where the tension and aggressive feelings had gone, the change in mood being totally mysterious and humanly incomprehensible. On that day and the days following I found the strength to care for Judith. She has made great progress. She is a beautiful girl who has helped me to grow. For me, her face is a daily presence of God and an expression of God's wish to see us grow together.

L'Arche, Honduras

🕊 You Sure Look Funny

The bishop of Winnipeg came for an evening meal.

Trevor: Where is your big hat?

Bishop: I left it at home, Trevor. I just wear it for special occasions.

Trevor: You sure look funny when you wear your hat. You should wear it all the time.

L'Arche, Winnipeg

🍀 The Protector

It was a time of deep political unrest and insecurity. There were shootings every night and death squads on the rampage in our neighborhood. Annette, the director, called a meeting of everyone in the house to reflect on what was happening and comfort those who were frightened. Justine, who has limited powers of expression, pointed her finger to the chapel and said, "We don't need to be afraid. Jesus in here." It was true, and to date we have been safe in his care.

L'Arche, Haiti

🍀 Global Village

We received a telegram that said, "Welcome aboard. You are one of us." It was official notice that we were accepted into L'Arche. We wondered how to express the notion of extended communities to members of our house. Eddie, who is deaf, saw the telegram on the bulletin board and signed at once: "Friends around the world."

L'Arche, Seattle

🐛 Gooseberry Tale

Picking strawberries that day in June was hot and boring. Don, a new assistant at Daybreak, was trying with only limited success to get Peter involved in the job. The best approach, we told Don, was to be loving but firm. It was clear that Peter just didn't enjoy it. He didn't complain; in fact, Peter rarely spoke at all. His form of protest was to sit on the strawberry plants, leaving a red stain spreading across his trousers. At last Don took his hand, pulled him to his feet, and looking directly into his eyes (since Peter didn't see well) said: "Peter, if *I'm* going to pick strawberries, *you're* going to pick strawberries. So let's get going!" Peter nodded and mumbled, "What's good for the goose is good for the gander." And he picked.

L'Arche, Toronto

🐛 Dialogue Mass

I go to Canterbury every Monday to celebrate mass. When we come to the point before com-

munion where I say "Peace be with you," Dean is usually ready to chip in with an offbeat remark. "Pleased to see you," he responded one time. Kind of an inspirational reply.

L'Arche, England

🐾 Bountiful Creation

Maressa's after dinner prayer: "O God, I just thank you for me."

L'Arche, Winnipeg

🐾 The Price of Growing Older

Janet's family came over to surprise her on her birthday, bringing ice cream and cookies. When Janet came downstairs the family shouted "Happy Birthday! Surprise!" Janet looked at Lisa and Lucy and said, "Does this mean I can't watch 'Golden Girls' tonight?"

L'Arche, Overland Park, Kans.

❧ Gift Passed On

John found it difficult to receive me. Often when we took walks together I would find something along the road and give it to him, but when that happened he usually threw the gift away. One day I picked a beautiful flower and presented it to him. On this particular day he looked at me and smiled. About ten yards down the road was a letter box. John carried the flower to the letter box, opened it and left the flower inside.

L'Arche, England

❧ Broken World

During the Gulf War Dennis prayed, "Please put the world back together."

L'Arche, Tacoma

🐦 A Basic Relationship

We were traveling to a regional gathering of L'Arche in Canada, which for Americans required birth certificates in order to clear Canadian customs. Everything was fine until we arrived at customs in Edmonton. Then Shawn revealed he had left his birth certificate at home because he didn't want to lose it. The customs agents were kind, but firm. We, for our part, were equally determined not to be sent back. When I explained why Shawn didn't have his birth certificate, a customs officer asked both of us to go to a side room.

Customs Officer: What is your relationship to this lady?

Shawn: Christella is my friend. We live together and we are going to live together forever.

Customs Officer: What is your relationship with this young man?

Christella: Shawn is my friend. We live together and we are going to live together forever.

We were released to proceed with our journey.

L'Arche, Overland Park, Kans.

❧ Perception

I was busy preparing for guests who were coming for a meeting. Pat, a disabled person, pulled out a chair for me to sit down. He remarked, "You're a bit anxious about all this, aren't you?"

L'Arche, Winnipeg

❧ They Are the Ones

Leonard sent me to the grocery store for pipe tobacco with the usual amount of money. But this time I returned emptyhanded, since inflation had caught up with Leonard's purse. When I had to announce to Leonard that prices had gone up and that I needed more money, he exploded: "What do you mean 'prices have gone up'? They're the ones who stick those things [price tags] on them." What could I tell him? My understanding of economics was barely more sophisticated than his.

L'Arche, Quebec

❧ Who Is There?

Dovie has been a community member since 1978 and during that time had experienced many comings and goings. Each one was painful for her. Dovie and I met to pray and share our life in community during one period when many assistants seemed to be leaving. As she was describing one particular loss, tears welled up in her deep brown eyes and spilled over. Together we cried, blew our noses and ran out of tissues. Suddenly there was a change of mood. Dovie became so angry there were darts coming from her eyes. "Jo, who is there?" she demanded. Confused, I said, "I don't understand." Dovie persisted: "Jo, who is there for me? You have Pat and your girls, but me—who is there for me?" Her question pierced me like an arrow. Who was there for Dovie? Who would be for Dovie until death? Choked, I answered, "Dovie, I don't know." Together we held one another and wept.

L'Arche, Calgary

❧ Is God As Good?

Sucaja, 13 years of age, enters the confessional. Minutes later she comes out, radiant. "The priest kissed me. Oh, how kind he is!" Then she asked, "Does that mean God is as good as he is?"

L'Arche, Honduras

❧ Resting in Order

Pat and I traveled to a distant cemetery so he could visit his grandparents' graves. I had never been there before, but Pat claimed he knew the location of the plots. On arrival he bolted from the car. But when after a lengthy search in the bitter cold weather we still hadn't found the gravesites, Pat suggested, "Maybe the graves are in order like the alphabet."

L'Arche, Overland Park, Kans.

✿ Means of Transportation

Sitting at the breakfast table one morning, I remarked that I had an important meeting to attend that day but no car to get me there. Several suggestions were put forward—borrow a car, take a bus, hitch a ride with our farm team—all of which I turned down for various reasons. To all of this Dave listened as he munched his cereal and rocked back and forth. Suddenly he slapped the table and gave the solution: "Sue, if you really need to go to the meeting, why don't you just ride your broomstick?"

L'Arche, Toronto

✿ Gift of God

At a birthday celebration for a fellow resident, Bill declared: "God so loved the world that he sent us Fred."

L'Arche, England

✦ Requiem

When Michael's grandmother died, his mother felt unable to cope both with her grief and his epileptic problems, so he wasn't told the news until he went home the weekend after the funeral. His father took him to one side as soon as Michael arrived. In the other room, he found his mother resting in bed. Without speaking he simply sat by her side and held her hand for almost forty-five minutes—a service of comfort, she said, that was precisely what she needed.

But Michael wasn't done. Noticing a silver vase, he haltingly asked his father to take out its flowers and fill the vase with Coca-Cola. It took some convincing from Michael, who stutters and finds it hard to speak his mind, but at last his father did as Michael requested. Michael, in the meantime, arranged three chairs and a small table on which was set the vase and a slice of bread. He placed his parents on one side of the table and himself on the other. "Now," Michael announced, "we will pray for Grandma." Breaking the bread, he handed pieces to each of his parents and asked them to pray, then took a piece himself and prayed aloud for his grandmother. The action was repeated with the vessel of Coke. When they had all prayed again, consumed the bread and drunk from the vase, Michael ended the ceremony by declaring that God would surely look after Grandma. The three of them, he said, must now begin to think of Grandpa who was alone and who needed their support.

L'Arche, Toronto

🐾 Gone But Still Here

Bill and Frank were dying. The community at Daybreak took a long time to decide whether they could stay in the house to the very end. We were worried that the deaths of these beloved friends under our own roof would have a negative impact on other core members. A special concern was for Annie whose father was dying around the same time. We shouldn't have worried. Throughout the long struggle of Bill and Frank, Annie was a constant companion at their bedsides, sharing her giggles with them almost as much as she shared her tears, and always whispering words of love to her "two honeys." After nearly two years, Frank was the first to go. With much trepidation, we approached Annie and told her that Frank had died. She wept, then looked up, clear-eyed and peaceful. "Frankie's gone," she said. "Can't see Frankie any more." Then tapping her chest, she added: "But Frankie's *here* now, here in my *heart!*" And so Annie, who we feared might be too fragile, showed us how to accept death with faith and joy.

L'Arche, Toronto

🐾 One of the Crowd

To celebrate the foundation of a new monastery just outside the city, Trappist monks held an open house and invited our community to attend. In a welcoming talk, a monk remarked that the lives of the monks are still modeled on that of St. Benedict. Maressa volunteered, "My Daddy knows St. Benedict." The monk was puzzled. "Your Daddy knows St. Benedict?" "Yes," said Maressa, "because my Daddy is in heaven."

L'Arche, Winnipeg

❧ Turnaround

Christina came to us when she was 18, a beautiful young woman with multiple medical problems and a victim of years of instability, abuse, family breakdown, neglect and isolation. When she first arrived she was bewildered and insecure, afraid of failure and desperately wanting to belong. She clung physically to everyone she met. She referred to people as Mom, Dad or Auntie. When demands were placed on her at home or at school, her invariable reply was an emphatic "I can't do it!" That was two years ago. Now, at 20, Christina has grown more peaceful. She no longer holds on to people. She feels better about herself and is more willing to take responsibility and risks. She has slowly come to realize she has a home, friends, and a measure of control over her life. Christina belongs.

L'Arche, Nova Scotia

🐾 Captured and Liberated

Dougie suffered from Huntington's Chorea. He and I used to play a little game when I visited him in an institution: I would get up to leave and Dougie would follow me in his walker, herding me into a corner to "capture" me. The game helped to cement our friendship. Often I would ask, "Where does God live?" Dougie, who gradually lost the ability to walk and then to talk, would point to the heavens. I wanted him to know God lives in our hearts. On the day he was baptized I asked him again, "Where does God live?" With his small hand permanently folded into a fist, he struck his chest and smiled.

Dougie died in my arms. We placed his body on a couch in the dayroom and invited the other disabled persons in to say goodbye. One by one they looked at Dougie, touched him, talked to him. Among the visitors was Morton, an older man with a deformed body. Morton placed his hands on Dougie. "Well, Dougie," he said, "you must go home now. I always thought of you as my son." There was only profound silence after that.

Rainier School, Tacoma

67

🐾 How We Will Know Him

Ross was a man in his mid-thirties. Although not a Catholic, he often celebrated mass with us. One day I ate with Ross in the lunchroom, and when we were done there was a piece of bread partly on his plate, partly on mine. He broke it, dividing it in half, looked at me and folded his hands in prayer.

I asked Ross what he was doing. He said, "This is what you do."

"You mean at church?

Ross answered, "You break the bread."

I probed some more. "Ross, what does that mean? Does it make you feel close to Jesus when you do that?"

He looked at me as if I didn't understand. "No, it makes me closer...I'm already close to Jesus."

It dawned on me: Ross understood.

Ranier School, Tacoma

❧ The Value of Friendship

Ricky was one of thirty disabled children who attended a diocesan summer camp. For much of his life Ricky had to wear a football helmet for protection against violent seizures, and even now he was severely limited in what he could do. Nevertheless, he was able to go swimming, and when he got chilly in the water the two of us sat on the grass and talked. At last he grew silent. I asked him what he was thinking about, expecting him to mention the out-of-doors, the water, the trees or the sky. Instead, Ricky answered, "Jesus."

"What do you think about Jesus?" I asked again.

"Jesus is my friend," he said simply. "He helps me to do everything I do."

It was my turn to be silent. Here was a boy who would never do anything on his own, never live by himself, never know independence, never be free of seizures, yet who rejoiced in the secure belief that Jesus was his friend.

L'Arche, Tacoma

🐾 Everything's Okay

Paul was in his mid-twenties. In addition to being developmentally disabled and a victim of strokes, he was a hemophiliac whose blood transfusions had led to his contracting AIDS. Despite his many afflictions, Paul faced his approching death serenely. We wondered how he managed it. About two weeks before his death, two of us were sitting at Paul's bedside and I asked him if he was okay. "Okay?" he responded, and looking at the assistant by his side asked, "Do you love me?" She was startled but replied that she did love him—that the care she gave him was a sign of her love. Turning to me, Paul asked, "Does God love me?" I answered him that God surely loved him. Then Paul said: "Well, if you love me and God loves me, I'm okay."

Ranier School, Tacoma

🐾 From Follower to Leader

While preaching a retreat for L'Arche core members, I made two major points: First, we should not be fearful, since Jesus promised "Don't be afraid. I am with you always." Second, Jesus invites us to follow him just as he invited the disciples. I attempted to drive these points home by using my listeners' names—"Louise, come, follow me. Francis, come, follow me. Hughette, come, follow me." Did they understand? They said they did. The next morning I was approached by Robert, a fervent and prayerful man, who confided, "Gilles, yesterday I prayed to Jesus and I told *him*, 'Don't be afraid. Come, follow me.'"

L'Arche, Quebec

🐾 Holy Cookie Monster

The eucharist was important to Melvin. When he came to mass each Wednesday evening, the first thing he asked was "Do I get the holy cookie tonight?" On first hearing it, I was taken aback, but eventually I came to feel "holy cookie" is a wonderful description of the eucharist.

Ranier School, Tacoma

🐾 The Therapist

Armando cannot walk or talk and is very small for his age. He came to us from an orphanage where he had been abandoned. He refused food because he no longer wanted to live cast off from his mother. He was desperately thin and dying for lack of food. After spending time in our community where people held him, loved him and wanted him to live, Armando began to develop in a remarkable way. He still can't walk, talk or eat by himself; his body is twisted and he has a severe disability. Yet when he's picked up his eyes glow and his whole body quivers with joy. He has a therapeutic influence on everyone in the community.

L'Arche, Rome

🐾 Good Friday

Barbara was the second of four children, three of whom have a disease called Batten Syndrome. Victims of Batten's are normal until about seven years old, then they begin to go blind. By ten or eleven they start to experience seizures, gradually losing the ability to walk. Finally they're confined to bed, trembling with almost constant seizures, although they never lose their sense of hearing.

I used to visit Barbara at her home, inevitably greeted when I came in by a big smile. One Good Friday I decided to read the passion to her. I was sitting next to her bed. Barbara was smiling, but as the story progressed she became very quiet, peaceful, and her body stopped shaking. When I got to the part about Jesus taking up his cross, Barbara raised both of her arms toward the ceiling. She made no sound. Her eyes left me as she gazed up in the direction of her arms. She did not have a seizure in a long time. When the passion account reached the death of Jesus, she took her arms down, laid them across her chest and closed her eyes. We stayed there in silence. At last one tear emerged from the corner of her eye and ran down her cheek. That Good Friday I knew I was in the presence of the suffering Jesus.

Ranier School, Tacoma

✿ Roommates

One night we were watching a television special when Suzy said she "had things to think about" and went to her room. The next day her mother called and asked if she worked things out. Suzy answered, "You know me and my memories. Sometimes I think of Grandma. I feel like she's in my room, and I just talk to her and it makes me feel better."

L'Arche, Overland Park, Kans.

✿ Everything's Okay

Acefie, a young staff member, died in our house two months after she had been diagnosed as having cancer of the liver. She wanted to stay with us until the end, and each member of the community helped in whatever way possible. After the funeral some members of her family stopped by for a visit. Before they even got to the door Yveline went up to them and declared: "You don't need to cry. We all took care of Acefie. I heated water for her, Jacqueline bathed her, Sylvie fed her and now

74

she's in heaven with God her Father, so every-thing's okay." We stood in silence. There was no need to say anything more.

L'Arche, Haiti

✄ A Day at the Circus

Each year someone in the house gets the pleasure of accompanying Craig to the circus, better known by him as the "Lircus." The morning when my turn came it was pouring rain. We had to walk several blocks to get to our car, and by the end of the first block we were drenched. I was cold and miserable. Craig, however, was smiling and happy, water streaming down his face.

"Craig, you're soaked," I said. "Are you okay?"

"Yeah," he said, and then broke into his favorite song: "Singing in the rain, I'm singing in the rain. What a beautiful feeling, I'm happy again! A root ta ta ta, a root ta ta ta, a root ta ta ta!" I couldn't help joining in. Suddenly the day took on a new life as we slogged along, singing and happy. Craig had a way of changing my perspective.

At last we made it to the car and sped off to the circus. Since we were late, we had to park in the driveway of a woman who was renting spaces to circus-goers.

Craig tugged at me. "Com'on, Karen, let's go to the Lircus!"

"Wait a minute," I said, "I have to pay."

Scrounging through my purse for $2.00, I could see the small, old woman watching me with distrust. "We're late for the circus," I explained. "May we pay afterward?"

The woman was unsure. "You come back? You promise? You pay $2.00?" Craig was yanking on my arm as the woman followed us. "You come back? You pay?"

All at once Craig stopped and went back to her. He put his hands on her shoulders, gazed into her eyes and said, "It's okay. It's okay." He stood with her for a moment, then grabbed me and whisked me down the street. The woman looked after us, quietly reassured.

The circus turned out to be everything Craig wanted: lions, tigers, popcorn and Coke. A happy man, he headed for the car while I went to pay the woman. But when I handed her the money, she pushed it away. "You give it to the boy," she said. She paused, and added: "You ask him to pray for me."

L'Arche, Vancouver

🐌 Lost and Found

A few months after I arrived in the community at Compeigne, I received a call from my
parents. My dad was seriously ill with an
infection in his heart and needed immediate
surgery. I asked everyone in the house to pray
for my father and made plans to fly home the
next day. Later that same afternoon we could-
n't locate Jacques, who is disabled. It wasn't
like him to disappear. Anxiously we searched
everywhere we could think of, without success. Two hours after we first missed him, he
showed up again. When I asked where he had
gone, he said, "I went to mass to pray for your
dad because he is sick."

L'Arche, France

🐌 What I Really Want

It had been a bad week at the woodworking
shop. Because it was Friday the whole crew
set off to the local diner for lunch. Joe was
tired and didn't want to go. Reluctantly he

approached the car and got in, but he was dragging. As he started the engine, David's big hands came over the front seat and began to massage his shoulders with great care and tenderness. Joe was deeply touched. After a moment he said, "Dave, if you continue doing that I'll have to give you a raise." Dave replied, "Joe, I don't want a raise. I just want to be with you." For Joe, it was his most precious moment at L'Arche.

L'Arche, Toronto

☙ Smart Request

Kenneth had a great talent for imitating his three favorite television characters: Batman, Superman and Maxwell Smart. He was new to L'Arche, arriving four weeks before Easter, so he wasn't prepared for the lean fare we served on Good Friday, a day of fast and abstinence. He watched as a bowl of soup, a slice of bread and a glass of water were placed on the table in front of him. He sank back in his chair, deflated, then pulled off his shoe and went into his Maxwell Smart routine. Just for his own amusement, he poked the heel of his shoe a few times with an index finger, waited, and said, "Yeah, can you send me over a burger and fries?"

L'Arche, Seattle

🕊️ Mustard Seed

The parable of the mustard seed—the smallest of seeds which grows into a tree large enough for birds to build their nests—came to life for me in the person of Vincent.

Vincent is a severely disabled child, blind, epileptic and almost completely paralyzed. Getting one thumb into his mouth is the only coordinated movement he can make. His brain is smaller than normal. He will never walk or talk and must depend on outsiders for all his care. In the eyes of society, Vincent is the smallest and weakest of seeds.

Vincent was six years old when I was asked to take care of him. I bathed him, dressed him, fed him and changed his diapers (job-training I never received in the Jesuit novitiate). I was Vincent's assistant.

Evening prayer each day was a privileged time for me and all the assistants at L'Arche

L'Etoile. The children we cared for were so severely disabled that communication was accomplished mostly by touching, and evening prayer offered a special opportunity for that. Resting comfortably in the arms of their assistants, the children would gradually fall asleep to the sound of soft music, and in this atmosphere they would come to know something of God's compassion and tenderness. And so would we.

On Pentecost Sunday there were only four of us at home, Vincent and I and little Helene, a fragile, profoundly handicapped girl, with her assistant. We were preparing for mass in the small chapel that had cushions on the floor and a low table that served as an altar. Helene was in her assistant's arms. I placed Vincent on cushions and was settling myself on the floor next to the altar when it occurred to me that it wasn't right for Vincent to be alone. So I picked him up and placed him next to me, with my left arm around him and his legs under the table. My right hand was free for the missal, the bread and the cup.

At the consecration of the bread something happened inside me. It's hard to explain. I was holding the bread in my right hand and I said the words, "This is my body..." Right then I was holding Vincent in my left, and it seemed that Jesus was telling me, "This is my body..." It made a perfect circle, the same reality, the same Presence. Vincent's body, so broken and poor, was also the broken body of Jesus. I held both in my hands, and I knew both of them were sacred.

I have a difficult time explaining what happened, but I can truly say something changed in me. Since then, I have never touched Vincent's body—whether bathing him, feeding him or changing his diapers—without feeling enormous respect, as if I touched something sacred. I feel the same about the broken bodies of Helene, William and John. Their sacredness is a mystery. Like Christ hidden in the eucharistic bread, it escapes our eyes and intelligence, but it nourishes our hearts.

For the world, Vincent remains a small, weak creature, like a mustard seed. But to me he has already become a great tree that bears fruit and where birds come to build their nests. Those who come close to him can touch the mystery of their hearts and approach the mystery of the heart of Jesus.

L'Arche, Quebec

🍀 According to Plan

One day Mary Francis, who recently arrived at our house, was making herself a handful for a very new assistant. "Mary Francis, you're driving me crazy!" exclaimed the assistant. "That's my plan," said Mary Francis.

L'Arche, Seattle

🍀 Three-Time Winner

Benoit is an autistic man who came to Lalla Mariam four years ago. He loves his birthday. For months prior to the day he tells us what presents he wants, who will be invited to his party and what they'll eat for dinner. He also has a wonderful memory and can tell you who came to his party in 1978 and what presents he got. This year during prayer time Benoit prayed, "Thank you, God, that I have celebrated my birthday three times."

L'Arche, France

🎕 The Ways of a Family

Marian is a beautiful lady of 54 who spent most of her life in an institution. The moment she saw me, when I came in the door, she told me she liked me and I believed her. That's the way Marian is. If she's happy she sings and laughs and makes the rest of us smile with her. If she's sad or unhappy she tells us, and usually cries. She's honest with her feelings, never holding them back. Letting my feelings show has always been hard for me, but Marian is teaching me how to do it.

I always thought that being a family meant creating a home—and family is what we are at Waycobah House. However, I've learned that "family" is much more than just "creating home." Family is sticking together when things get tough or when one of us is going through a hard time. All of us are disabled in some way, and to be a family we must take off our masks and recognize our limitations. Only then do we begin to appreciate each other for who we are and not for who we try to be.

From my experience it's the core members who keep our community together. Buddy's joy, Tammy's noises, Susan's smiles, Rufus' secret handshake and Marian's singing mean family for me. They're the ones who love first, who accept first, who forgive first and who let go first. I came to L'Arche figuring I would be the teacher, but it was the core members who taught me about living as a community.

L'Arche, Cape Breton, Nova Scotia

❧ Extra Thoughtfulness

At the end of facilitating a community weekend, I was given a L'Arche Sudbury sweatshirt as a gift. I held up the lovely sweatshirt and said, "Oh good, XL." Some of the community members snickered, but Mary came to my rescue and said, "That means extra love."

L'Arche, Sudbury, Ont.

❧ A Word for It

One lazy summer afternoon an assistant was instructing Mary Francis in the ways of making bread. "Mary Francis, what do they call people who bake bread?" the assistant asked. "Loafers," replied Mary Francis.

L'Arche, Seattle

❧ Tom

Tom came to L'Arche about six weeks after I did. It was a sunny day in mid-October when he arrived carrying a cardboard suitcase and followed by two social workers. One of them handed over Tom's file, looked at the other and asked "Where shall we have lunch?" and they left. Tom stood there, his 5-foot 10-inch, 200-pound frame showing fear and confusion, not wanting to let go of his suitcase and gazing intently at his black digital wristwatch.

He was hungry. We told him he would eat as soon as we took him to the house where he would live, but Tom didn't want to get into our car. He pleaded with us, "Tom doesn't want to go back to Cedar Village. Nope, no more Cedar Village." We did our best to assure him he would never go back. For a long time after that, whenever he got into a car, we'd repeat the message: No more Cedar Village. The mystery of why Tom disliked Cedar Village was never solved during my time at L'Arche. It was one of the many secrets he couldn't tell us about, but if you listened carefully bits and pieces of Tom's thirty-three years in institutions would come to the surface. He carried the rest in his heart.

It took many months for Tom to realize that he truly had a new family at L'Arche. As the time passed, in fact, Tom got to the point where he wanted to ride in every car and couldn't understand when that was impossible. There were many disappointments in Tom's life.

His adjustment to new surroundings was a learning experience for Tom and me. For instance, he learned to live in a regular home where he didn't have to pay a quarter every time he wanted coffee (Tom loved coffee more than anything), and where he could turn bread into toast by putting it into this slot and pushing down that button. He could help himself to his own food at the table. His only problem was understanding that others liked mashed potatoes, too.

Tom expressed his likes and dislikes in very clear terms. He wanted to wear his blue cowboy shirt every day—the shirt that matched his clear blue eyes. He liked black digital watches on men's wrists, rings on women's fingers. He liked to touch bald heads and long, beautiful hair, and without hesitation would approach strangers to do it. What a challenge to walk with him through a crowded shopping mall!

Tom's favorite saying was, "Get out of the road!" He used the words for Ginger the dog, Scruffy the cat, for raindrops falling on his face or for stones in his path. Just across the road from our house was the Seine River, which was hardly more than a creek most of the year. Tom would pick up those irritating stones and hurl them into the water. Perhaps with each one he was discarding some part of his hurtful past. We were lucky we were never cited by Environment Canada for changing the course of the river.

Tom loved to laugh. I remember one particular occasion during Ash Wednesday services at one the biggest churches in Winnipeg. Inevitably, the longer the service the more laughter bubbled up from deep inside Tom. I was kneeling next to him, tugging at his sleeve to keep him quiet, while several elderly ladies in front shot disapproving glances in our direction. Their looks seemed to say, "Be quiet! Show respect!" Just in the second before Tom's mirth bubbled over I heard the celebrant say, "Happy are those who come to the table of the Lord." I thought to myself: Which one of us is truly following the words of Jesus? Who is truly showing respect? I'll always cherish that moment.

Bald heads! I learned not to be embarrassed with traveling with Tom. One day in a doctor's reception room, Tom noticed a man with the baldest, shiniest head imaginable. Before I could stop him, Tom began carressing the head with both hands. The man looked up, startled, and then grinned. "So you like my shiny head?" he asked. We all laughed. Tom shook hands with the man. I was grateful for the gentleman's understanding.

Along with his sense of humor, Tom had an uncanny knack of picking up people's mannerisms and imitating them. He could copy the way one person walked, the way another drank coffee or took snuff. If you tended to talk with your hands, you could count on seeing yourself in Tom. No mirror was necessary. He had a habit of walking behind a person and imitating their gait. After a minute he'd stop, slap his knee and double up with laughter.

Tom and I came to L'Arche together. The only difference between us was that I asked to come, he didn't. He shaped my life in many ways. Our growth of our spirits side-by-side created a fabric that stories are made of.

L'Arche, Winnipeg

❧ Healing Not Required

Jonas is a severe epileptic. One Sunday our community was sharing reflections about the fifth chapter of Luke's gospel, in which a man with leprosy approaches Jesus with the words, "Sir, if you want to, you can make me clean." In all of this, Jonas said nothing. Someone asked him, "Jonas, would you like to ask Jesus to heal you?" Jonas said "No." We were all shocked, but Jonas explained, "I'm okay. It's enough that Jesus supports me."

L'Arche, Haiti

❧ Just a Precaution

Every year when we prepare for advent, Suzy asks her famous question: "Why do we put a pink candle in the advent wreath?" Before anyone can answer, she replies, "Because they thought it might be a girl."

L'Arche, Overland Park, Kans.

❧ The Foundress

This is the story of Alexandria, affectionately called Xandu.

Before coming to L'Arche at the age of twelve, Xandu lived with her family but received no care from them. Her mother, who loved her, was blind and ailing. The rest of the family ignored or rejected her. She lived in abominable conditions, covered with her own feces which she sometimes ate. She was filled with rage and fear.

When Xandu came to live at L'Arche we sensed that she wanted to enter into relationships but was profoundly insecure. She could be violent with people smaller than she was, especially when they got attention before she did. She continually challenged our commitment to her. To get what she wanted she would become crazy, screaming and carrying on so violently that one day a neighbor came to see if we were beating her.

At first Xandu refused kisses, hugs or any sign of tenderness from us, but she also knew her behavior was inappropriate in this new home, and she would sometimes ask us to help her learn how to act. As caretakers we had to be firm but also consistent in the way we dealt with her, until eventually the limits we set gave her a sense of security and she began to take chances on her own. She wanted to be gentler with us. I remember we used to take her hand and show her how to stroke people and things lovingly. She was with us a year before she gave her first kiss. After that, the changes came quickly.

Xandu is now eighteen. She likes her body. She loves to take showers (although she still needs help) and adores wearing perfume. Her vocabulary is limited, but recently she has been asking the assistants "Do you love me?" and when they answer "yes" she bursts into laughter. Best of all, Xandu has become our teacher in the ways of welcoming—always delighted to open her arms and share hugs with other people. She dances, sings and has a healthy sense of humor.

How do you measure the value of a person's life? Perhaps Xandu will never be able to live on her own, and in the opinion of some her life is a waste. Xandu, however, is recognized as a founder of L'Arche in Brazil, and it is through her joy that we are united.

L'Arche, Brazil

AFTERWORD

Smiles are hidden in tears. Tears are hidden in smiles. This is true everywhere, but especially in L'Arche where pain and joy, sorrows and laughter, sadness and gladness are never separate.

The stories and anecdotes Christella Buser has collected in this little book show the meaning of Jesus' words, "your sorrows will be turned into joy." This joy is often understood as a joy after sorrow when all pain is over, but here we see how joy can shine through our pain.

The time for crying and the time for laughing is often the same time. Our tears are the voice that allows smiles to emerge from the soil of our broken lives.

In our society we are encouraged in many subtle ways to keep a thick wall between our sadness and our gladness, as if they were each other's enemies. But in L'Arche those who are considered marginal in society teach us that the cross is a place without walls between pain and joy, darkness and light, death and life. It is their teaching that brought me to L'Arche seven years ago and that keeps me here today.

When Bill, one of the members of our community, said to me, "If you die before I do I'll miss you a lot, and if I die before you do you'll miss me a lot," I felt the oneness of our pain and joys. I realized that we stood together under the cross, not despairing but full of hope.

Thank you, Christella, for collecting these precious little stories and anecdotes. They fill our eyes with tears and smiles, and we are better for them.

Henri J.M. Nouwen

THE HOMES OF L'ARCHE

Australia

L'Arche Sydney
PO Box 312
Burwood 2134 NSW

Beni Abbes
PO Box 132
Tasmania 7008

Genesaret
PO Box 734
Woden 2606
A.C.T.

Belgium

Aquero
14 rue St. Pierre
B-1301 Bierges

De Ark Antwerpen
Madona
Janssenei 12
B-2530 Bocchout

L'Arche Bruxelles

36A rue General Five
1040 Bruxelles

Le Murmure
49 rue du Chalet
4920 Aywaille

L'Arche Namur
Rue du Seminaire 11B
2e et locaux 236-237
5000 Namur

Brazil

Arca do Brasil
R. Manoel Aquillino dos
Santos 163
Vila Nova Cachocirinha
Jardin Eliza Maria
02873-520 Sao Paulo S.P.

Burkina Faso

Npmgr Maasem
01 BP 1492
01 Ouagadougou

Canada

L'Arche Agape
19 rue Front
Hull, Quebec JY8 3M4

L'Arche Ottawa
Maison Alleluia
889 Lady Ellen Place
Ottawa, Ontario KLZ 5L3

L'Arche Antigonish
97 Church Street
Antigonish, N.S. B2G 2E2

L'Arche Calgary
307-57 Avenue S.W.
Calgary Alberta T2H 2T6

L'Arche La Caravane
R.R. 2
Green Valley, Ontario
K0C 1L0

L'Arche Cape Breton
Whycocomagh,
Nova Scotia B0E 2K0

L'Arche Chinook*
14 Sherwood Cres. W.
Lethbridge, Alberta T1K
6G1

Daybreak
11339 Younge Street
Richmond Hill, Ontario
L4C 4X7

L'Arche Sudbury
66 Elm Street - Suite 300
Sudbury, Ontario P3A
1R8

L'Etoile
613 Hermine
Quebec G1N 2H2

Fleurs de Soleil
221 Bernard Pilon
Beloeil, Quebec J3G 1V2

L'Arche Arnprior
23 Lake Street
Arnprior, Ontario K7S
2Z9

L'Arche Hamilton
35 King Street East, 4
Hamilton, Ontario L8M
1A1

Homefires
P.O. Box 1296
Wolfville, Nova Scotia
B0P 1X0

L'Arche North Bay
240 Algonquin Avenue -
Suite 306
North Bay, Ontario P1B
4V9

L'Arche Mauricie
2174 6th Avenue
Trois-Rivieres, Quebec
G8Z 3B1

Le Printemps
100 route Frampton C.P.
66
St. Malachie, Quebec G0R
3N0

La Saule Fragile*
191 2nd Avenue West
Amos, Quebec J9T 1S4

L'Arche Stratford
82 Huron Street
Stratford, Ontario N5A
5S6

Shalom
7708 - 83rd Street
Edmonton, Alberta T6C
2Y8

Shiloah
7401 Sussex Avenue
Burnaby, British
Columbia V5J 3V6

L'Arche Victoria
1640 Gladstone Avenue
Victoria, BC V8R 1S7

* Probationary member

L'Arche Winnipeg
615 rue Laflèche
Winnipeg
MB R2J 0C9

L'Arche Montreal
6644 boulevard Monk
Montreal, Quebec
H4E 3J1

Denmark

Niels Steensens Hus
Nygade 6
DK 3000 Heisingor

Dominican Republic

Communidad del Area
Apdo 22279 El Huacal
Santo Domingo

France

Algrefoin
78470 St. Remy les
Chevreuse

L'Arc-en-ciel
11 rue Francois Mouthon
75015 Paris

L'Arche
BP 35 Trosly-Breuil
60350 Cuise-la-Motte

L'Atre
21 rue Obert
59118 Wambrechies

L'Arche Ecorcheboeuf
76590 Abbevukke-sur-Scie

Le Caillou Blanc
La Fabrique
Clohars Fouesnant
29118 Benodet

Le Levain
1 Place St. Clement
B.P. 316
60203 Compiegne Cedex

La Merci
16200 Courbillac
Jarnac

Moita
St. Germain
26390 Hauterives

Le Moulin de l'Auro
Chem de la Muscadelle
8400 L'Isle su la Sorque

L'Oliver*
30 rue de la Noe
35170 Bruz

La Rebellerie
49560 Nueil-sur-Layon

La Rose des Vents
Verpillieres
80700 Roye

La Ruisselee*
72220 St. Mars d'Outille
Ecomoy

Les Sapins
Les Abels
Lignieres-Sonneville
16130 Segonzac

Le Seneve
La Cariziere
44690 La-Hale-Fouassiere

Les Trois Fontaines
62164 Ambleteuse

La Vigne*
16 Rue de L'Est
21000 Dijon

La Croisee*
210 rue Roger Salergro
69100 Villeurbanne

Germany

Arche Regenbogen
Apfelallee 23
4542 Techklenburg

Arche Volksdorf
Farmsener Landstr. 198
D-22359 Hamburg

Haiti

L'Arche de Carrefour
BP 11075
Carrefour, Port-au-Prince

L'Arche Chantal
Zone de Cayes
CP 63 Cayes

Honduras

El Area de Honduras
Apartado 1273
Tegucigalpa DF

Communidad del Arca*
Casa san Jose
Apartado 241 Choluteca

Hungary

La Barka*
Arany JU 45
2330 Dunaharasti

India

Asha Niketan
53/7 Bannerghatta Road
Bangalore 560029

Asha Nikeltan
37 Tangra Road
Calcutta 700015

Asha Niketan
Nandi Bazaar P.O.
Katalur, Calicut DT
Kerala 673531

Asha Niketan
Kottivakkam
Tiruvanmiyur P.O.
Madras 600041

Ireland

L'Arche Cork
Le Cheile
Togher Road, Cork 4

L'Arche Dublin*
20 Duncarraig
Carrickbrack Road
Sutton, Dublin 13

L'Arche Kilkenny
3 Mill Street
Callan, Co. Kilkenny

Italy

Il Chicco
Via Ancona 1
00043 Ciampino
Roma

Ivory Coast

L'Arche de Bouake
04 BP 373
Bouake 04

Japan

Kana-no-ie*
Ashikubo
Kuchigumi 1255
421 21 Shizuoka-shi

Mexico

El Arca*
Apdo Postal 112-100
Sta. Martha Acatitla
Mexico 09510

Philippines

Punia
118 Camia Street
Bayianthan Village
Cainta Rizal

Poland

Arka
Sledziejowice 83
32020 Wieliczka

Arka*
ul Zytnia 34
61-625 Poxnan

Spain

El Rusc
Apartat 196
Tordera, Barcelona 08399

El Arca de Santa Maria*
c/Calders, s/n
08180 Moia

Switzerland

Im Nauen*
Oberdorfstr. 9
4146 Hochwald-Bale

La Carolle
26 Chemin d'Ecogia
1290 Versoix
Geneva

La Grotte*
Avenue Jean Gambach 26
1700 Fribourg

Uganda

Arche Uganda
P.O. Box 14095
Mengo-Kampala

United States

The Ark
402 South 4th Street
PO Box 230
Clinton, Iowa 52732

L'Arche Syracuse, 1701
James Street, Syracuse,
New York 13206

Community of the Ark
2474 Ontario Road NW
Washington, DC 200099-
2705

The Hearth
523 West 8th Street
Erie, PA 16502

Hope
151 S. Ann Street
Mobile, Alabama 36604

Irenicon
73 Lamoille Avenue
Bradford, MA 01835

L'Arche Cleveland
2634 E. 127th Street
PO Box 20450
Cleveland, OH 44120

L'Arche Heartland
PO Box 40496

Overland Park, KS 66204-
4493

Noah Sealth
816 15th Avenue East
Seattle, WA 98122-0023

L'Arche Spokane
223 E. Augusta Ave. #100
Spokane, WA 99207

Tahoma Hope
The Farmhouse
11716 Vickery Road East
Tacoma, WA 98446

L'Arche Nehalem*
107 S.E. 86th Avenue
Portland, OR 97216

Harbor House*
700 Arlington Road
Jacksonville, FL 32211-
7306

United Kingdom

L'Arche Liverpool
"The Ark Workshops"
Lockerby Road
Liverpool L7 0HG

L'Arche Bognor Regis
Goff House
Argyle Road, Bognor

Regis
West Sussex PO21 1DY

L'Arche Brecon*
Corlan y Bryn
120 Cradoc Close
Brecon Poways, Wales
LD3 9UB

L'Arche Inverness
Braerannoch
13 Drummond Crescent
Inverness, Scotland IV2
4QR

L'Arche Kent
Little Ewell
Barfrestone, Dover
Kent CT 15 7JJ

L'Arche Lambeth
15 Norwood High Street
West Norwood
London SE27 9JU

L'Arche Edinburgh*
18 Claremont Park
Leith
Edinburgh EH6 7PJ